W9-AZA-770

CHRISTMAS
IS COMING

For Natsu, Aki and Goh Hatayama, Nami and Nico Hirota, and Amy Gallant.

Activities in this book require scissors and/or a sharp-edged cutting tool such as a mat- or Exacto knife. Parental supervision is advised.

Text by B. Lancet

Special thanks to Shigeyoshi Suzuki, Barry Lancet, Michiko Uchiyama, and Miyoko and Michio Taniuchi.

Published by Kodansha International Ltd., 17-14 Otowa 1-chome, Bunkyo-ku, Tokyo 112, and Kodansha America, Inc. ★★ Distributed in the United States by Kodansha America, Inc., 114 Fifth Avenue, New York, New York 10011, and in the United Kingdom and continental Europe by Kodansha Europe Ltd., 95 Aldwych, London WC2B 4JF. ★★ Copyright © 1995 Tsuneo Taniuchi and Kodansha International. All rights reserved. Printed in China. First edition, 1995. ★★ LIBRARY OF CONGRESS CATALOGING-IN-PUBLICATION DATA: Taniuchi, Tsuneo, 1953– • a story and project book / Tsuneo Taniuchi.—1st ed. • Summary: A rhyming story counts down the last five days before Christmas, with instructions included for making the ornaments described in the rhyme. • 1. Christmas—Juvenile fiction. [1. Christmas—Fiction. 2. Stories in rhyme. 3. Christmas decorations. 4. Handicraft.] I. Title. • PZ8.3. T14544Ch   1955   [E]—dc20   95–21279 CIP AC

1 2 3 4 5 6 7 8 9 10   99 98 97 96 95   ISBN 4-7700-1990-4

Tsuneo Taniuchi

CHRISTMAS
IS COMING

A Story and
Activity Book

KODANSHA INTERNATIONAL

Tokyo • New York • London

It's five days before Christmas
And snow begins to fall.
Outside the sky grows dark. . . .
Silence settles over all.

Look! It's stopped snowing!
   Everything seems fresh and new.
It's going to be a white Christmas,
   and a beautiful one, too.

Up in the sky
    a star shines bright.
Now we *know* Christmas is coming,
    from the clear, yellow light.

Let's check the calendar,
   to see where we are.
Let's count down the days,
   it's not very far . . .

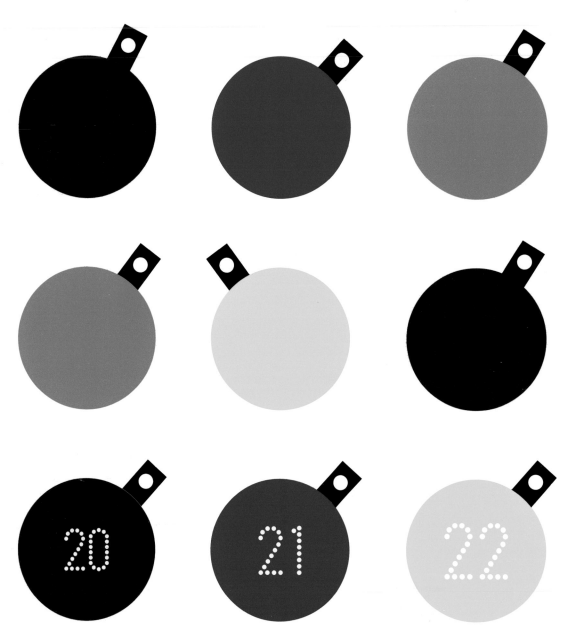

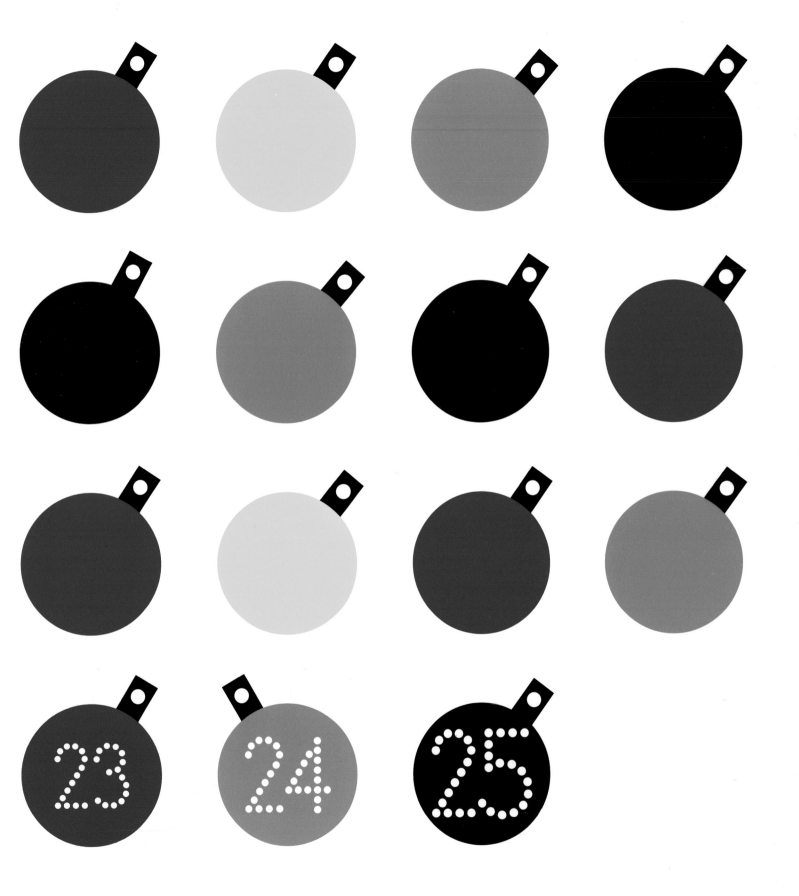

Today is the twentieth,
only five days left!
Let's hang some ornaments,
and make our tree the best!

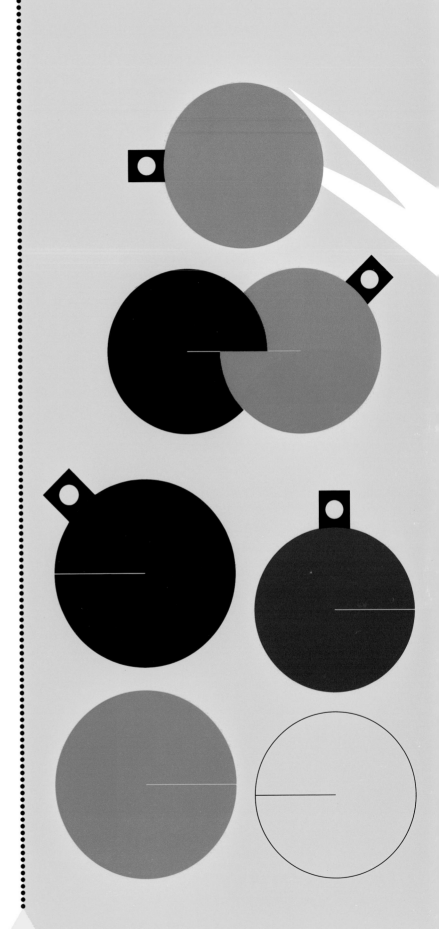

TO MAKE BALL ORNAMENTS

Cut out the two yellow fields along the dotted lines, then neatly snip out the circles. Carefully slit each circle along the line, punch out holes in black nodes at top, then slide two circles together at ninety-degree angles as shown on back side of this flap. Thread a piece of string through node hole, tie ends together to make a loop, then hang finished ornaments on tree.

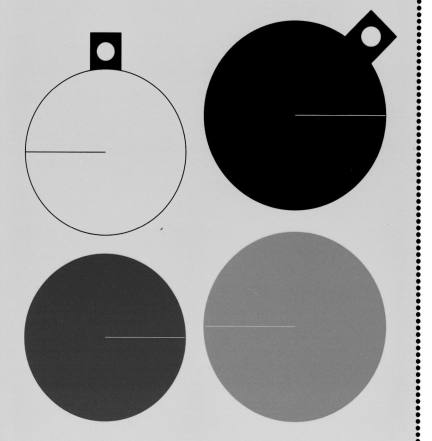

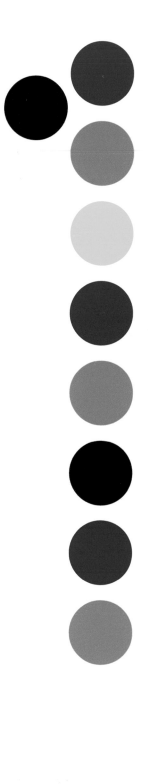

Christmas is coming,
just four more days. . . .

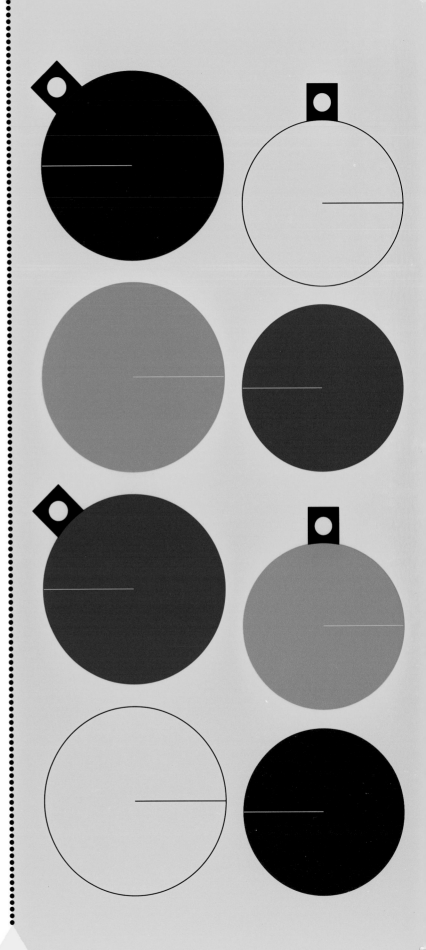

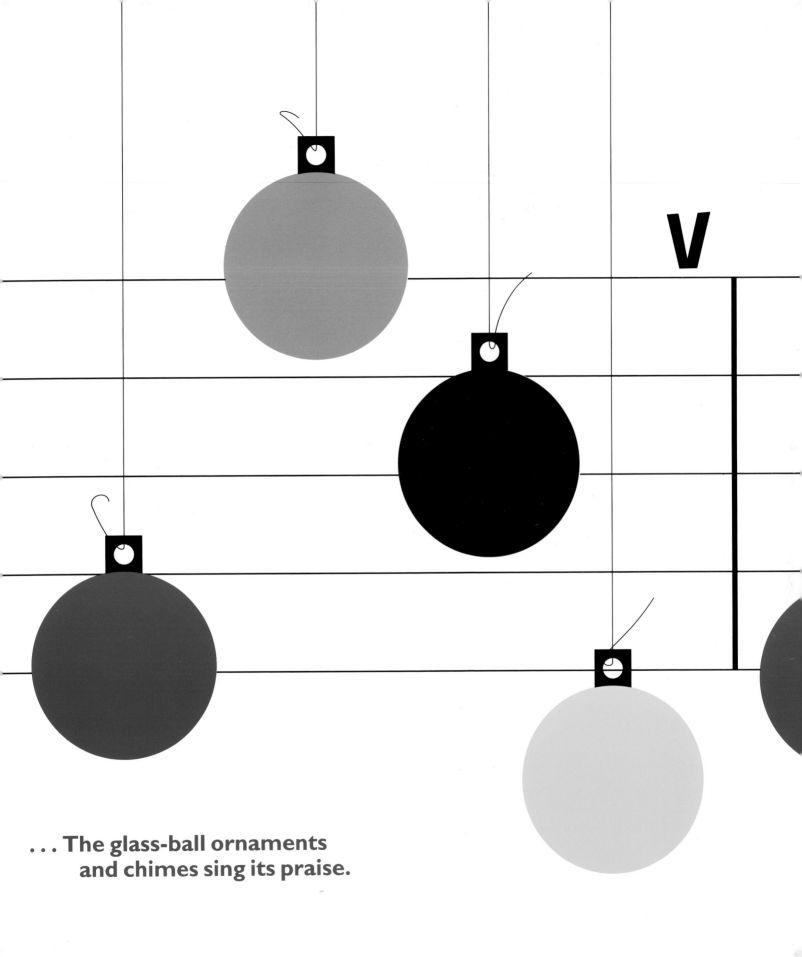

. . . The glass-ball ornaments
and chimes sing its praise.

When we think of Christmas,
we think of snow and stars,
And Santa and his reindeer,
who take him near and far.

Christmas is coming
  only three days to go.
Over there, from the window,
  I see a faint glow.

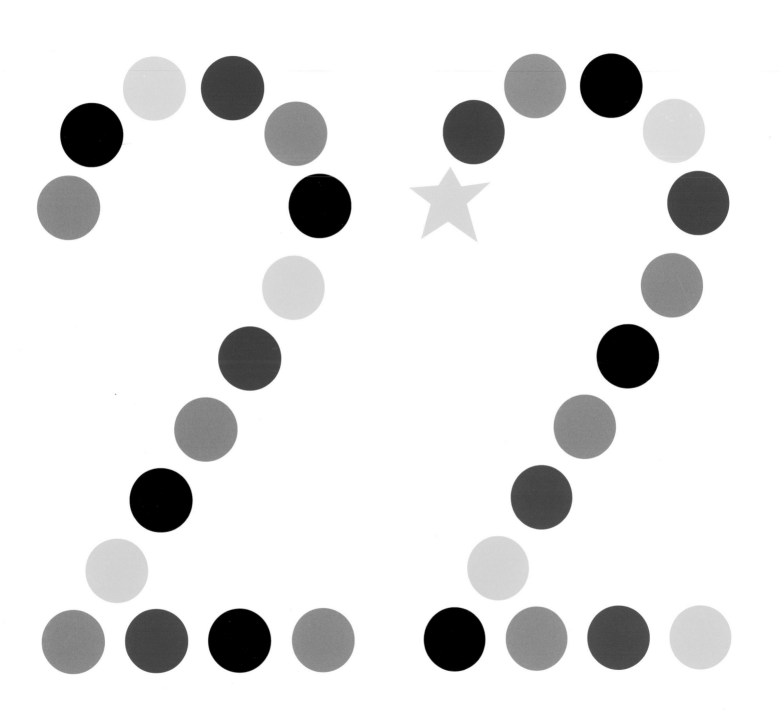

That gives me an idea
to use on the tree. . . .

TO MAKE STAR CLUSTER

Place a newspaper or blotter under star cluster to protect pages of the book underneath it. Cut out star cluster with a mat- or Exacto knife and carefully remove cluster from book page. Cut out and discard yellow sections. Score dotted lines between stars lightly with edge of knife, then fold stars down carefully along scored lines to a ninety-degree angle or less. Punch a small hole in center and pass a threaded needle through hole. Knot thread on both ends. Use finished cluster at the top of your Christmas tree, as a tree ornament, or as an independent mobile "hanging free."

. . . How about a star-cluster
hanging free?

Only two more days
until Santa arrives.
Have you been *very* good?
Did you tell any lies?

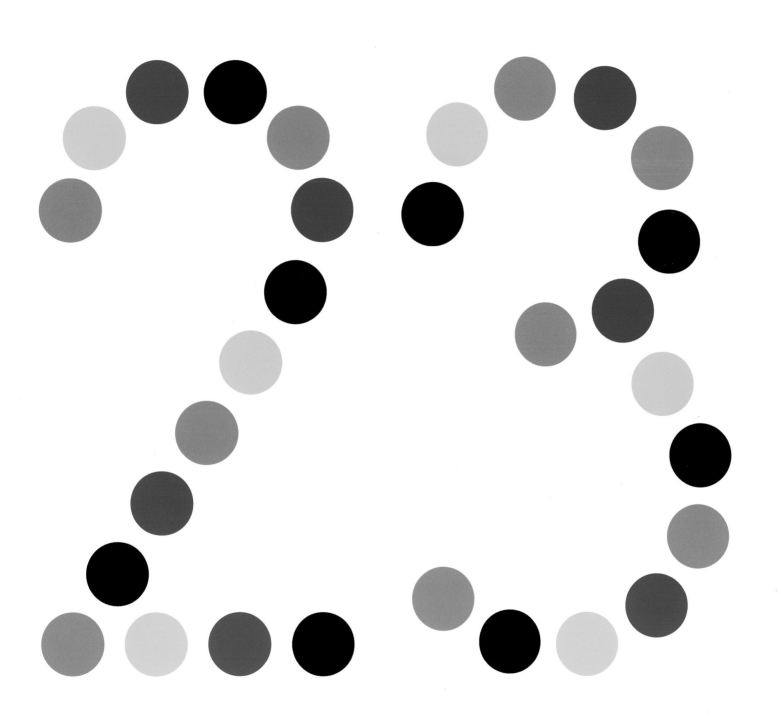

I hope not because . . .
    Santa always hears.
His reindeer, you know,
    have long, very large ears.

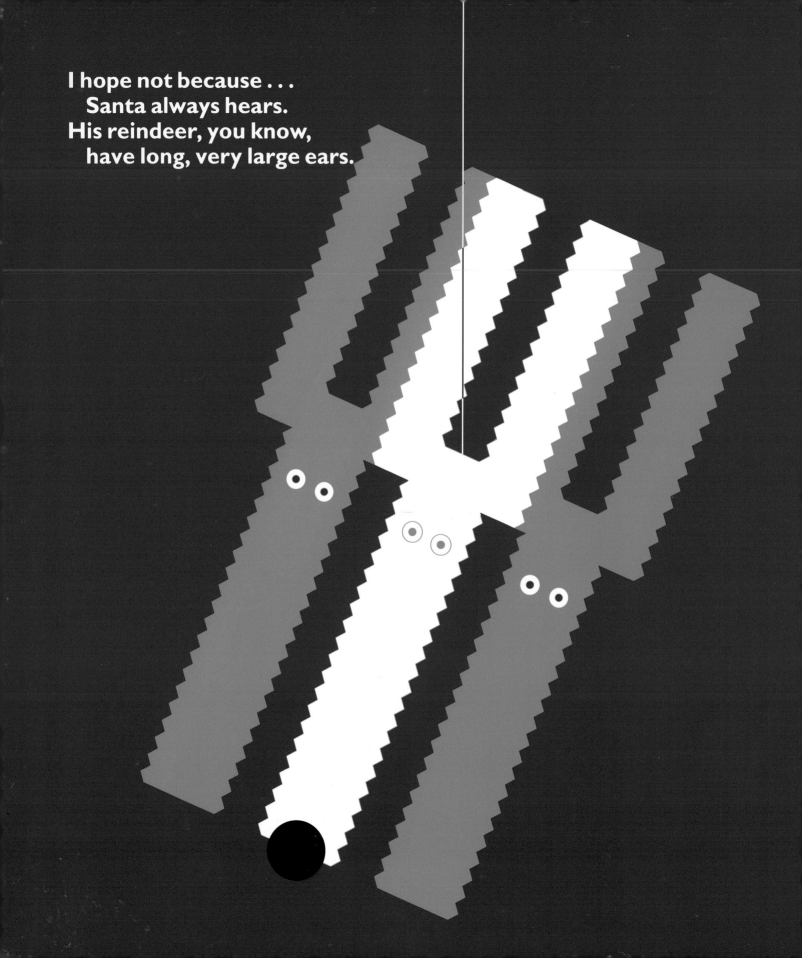

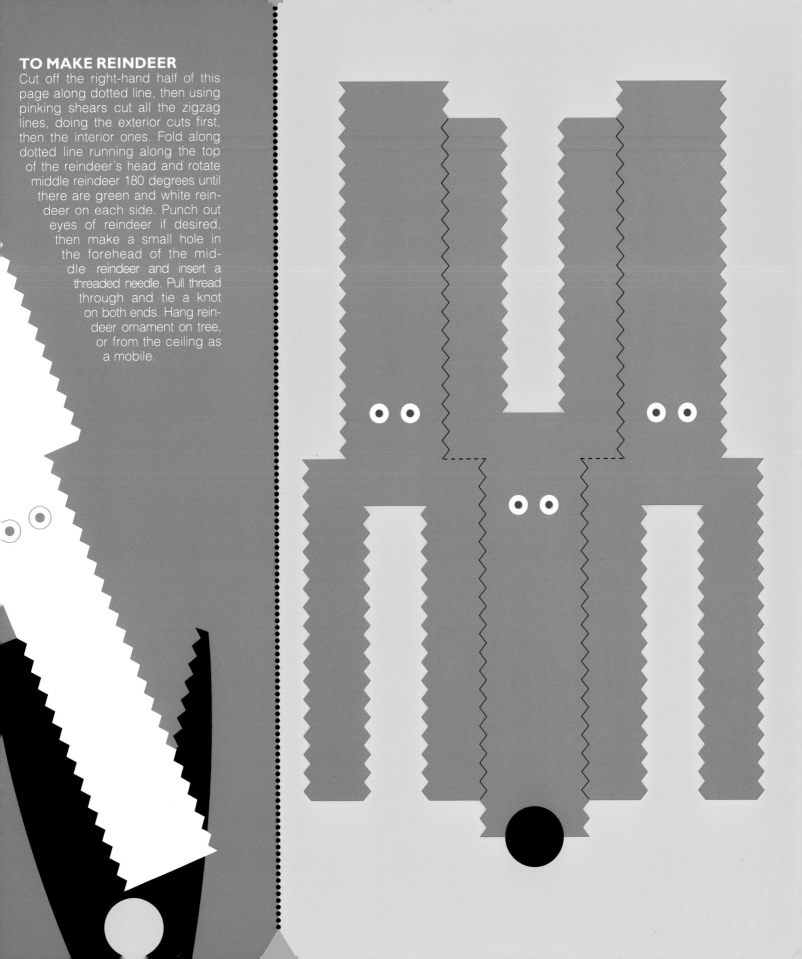

TO MAKE REINDEER
Cut off the right-hand half of this page along dotted line, then using pinking shears cut all the zigzag lines, doing the exterior cuts first, then the interior ones. Fold along dotted line running along the top of the reindeer's head and rotate middle reindeer 180 degrees until there are green and white reindeer on each side. Punch out eyes of reindeer if desired, then make a small hole in the forehead of the middle reindeer and insert a threaded needle. Pull thread through and tie a knot on both ends. Hang reindeer ornament on tree, or from the ceiling as a mobile.

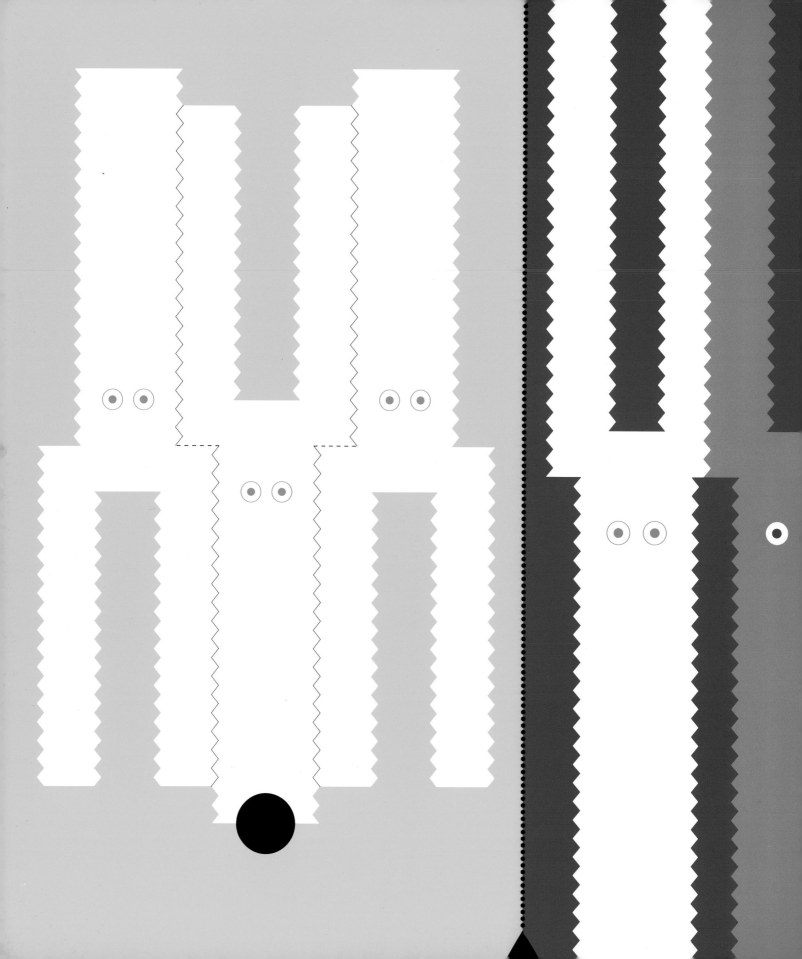

With the holiday at hand
   and in the air such good cheer,
Candlelight is perfect,
   helping bring Santa near.

TO MAKE SANTA
Cut out the yellow field along dotted line, then cut out Santa. Affix a piece of thread to back of head with a small piece of transparent tape and hang ornament on tree. TO MAKE A SPINNING TOY: Punch out the buttons, pass a three-foot piece of string through the buttonholes, and tie ends together to make a loop. Insert a finger into ends of string loop and pull tight to make Santa spin.

**Santa is coming,
reindeer are running.
And you know what that means . . .
Presents . . . incoming!**

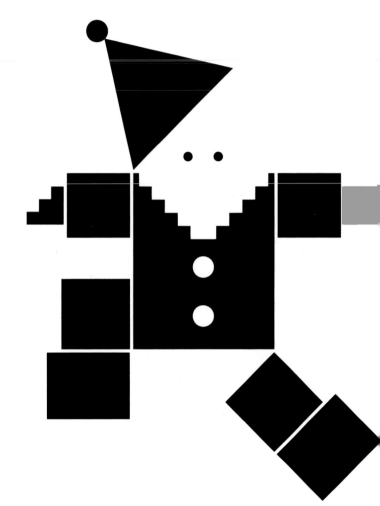

Santa flies everywhere
over land, over sea.
He stops at every house
bringing gifts—and glee.

He dances and prances,
sometimes even stumbles . . .

. . . But he always leaves presents,
neatly or in jumbles.

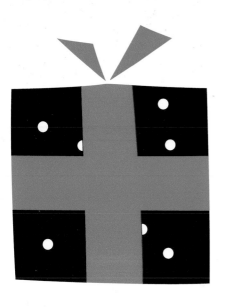

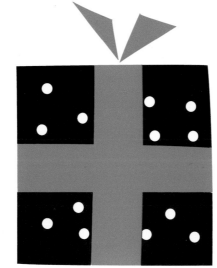

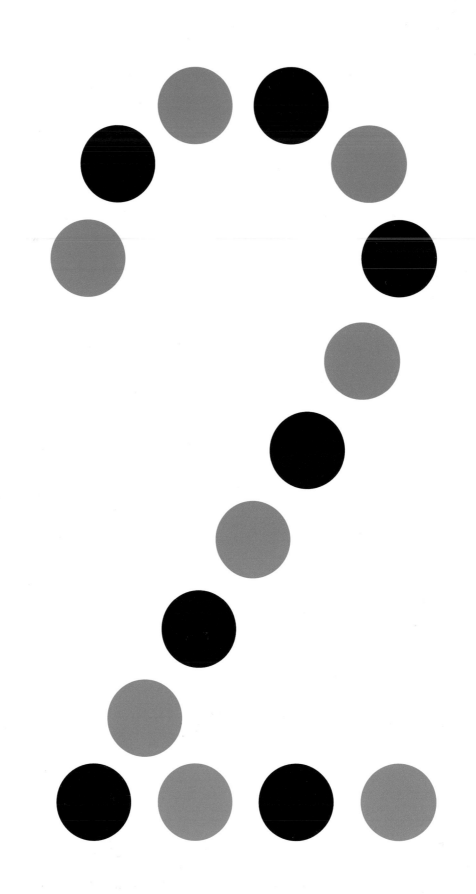

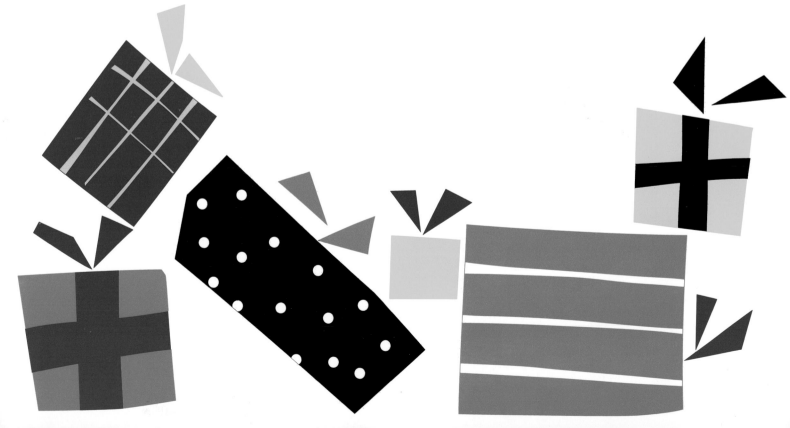

Santa was here
   last night, I know.
How could I tell?
   I heard his Ho-ho-ho.

The stockings are all emptied,
 the presents all opened.
It's time to go outside
 and build top-hatted snowmen.

TO MAKE SNOWMAN
Cut out snowman, then fold two matching halves over. Punch a small hole in top hat along fold. String, tie, and hang on tree.

With snowmen so jolly,
Christmas is complete.
Let's do it *all* again next year,
it will be such a treat!